Printed in the United States of America

ISBN 9781724401557

This book belongs to:

••••••••••••••••••••••

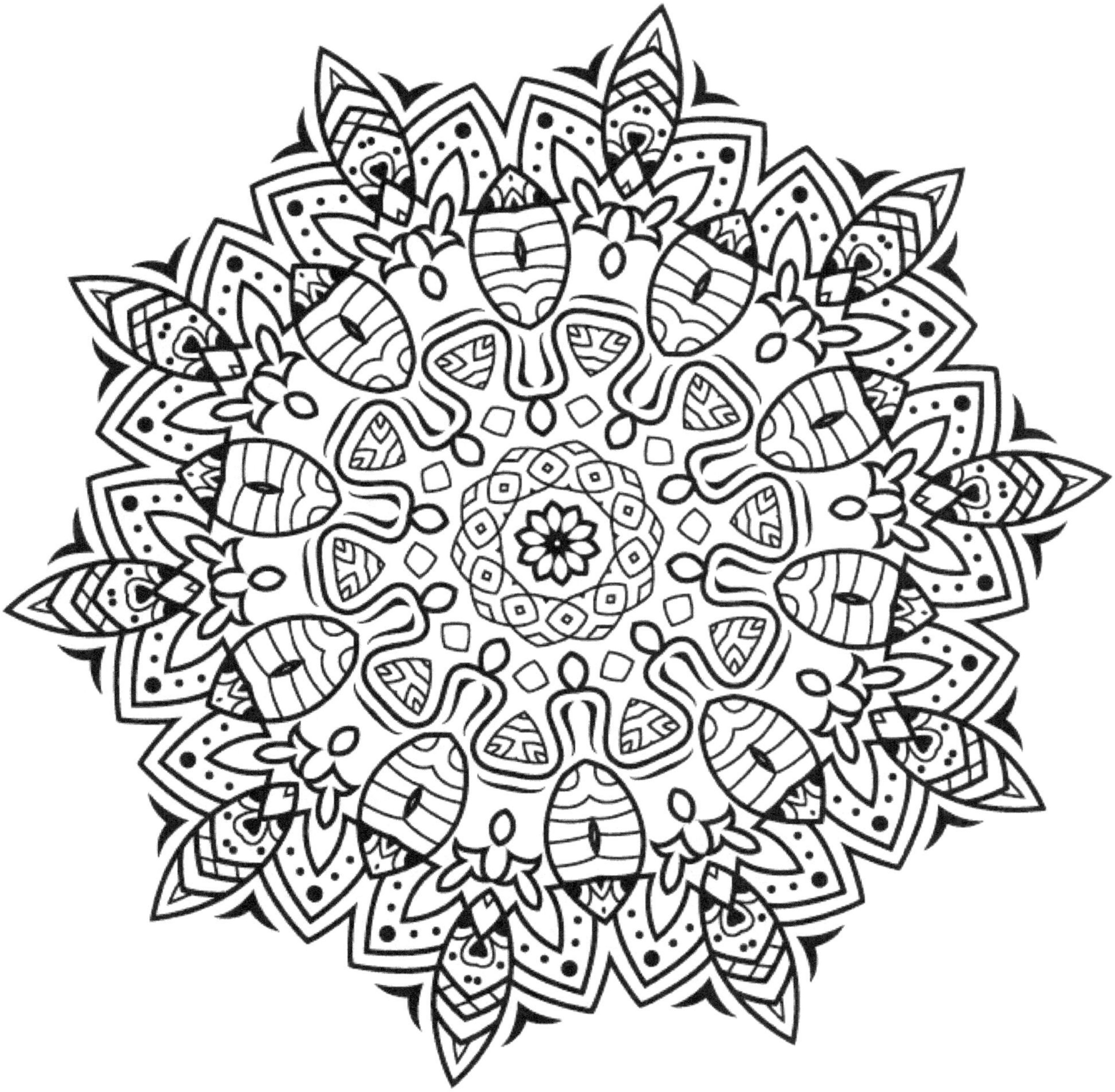

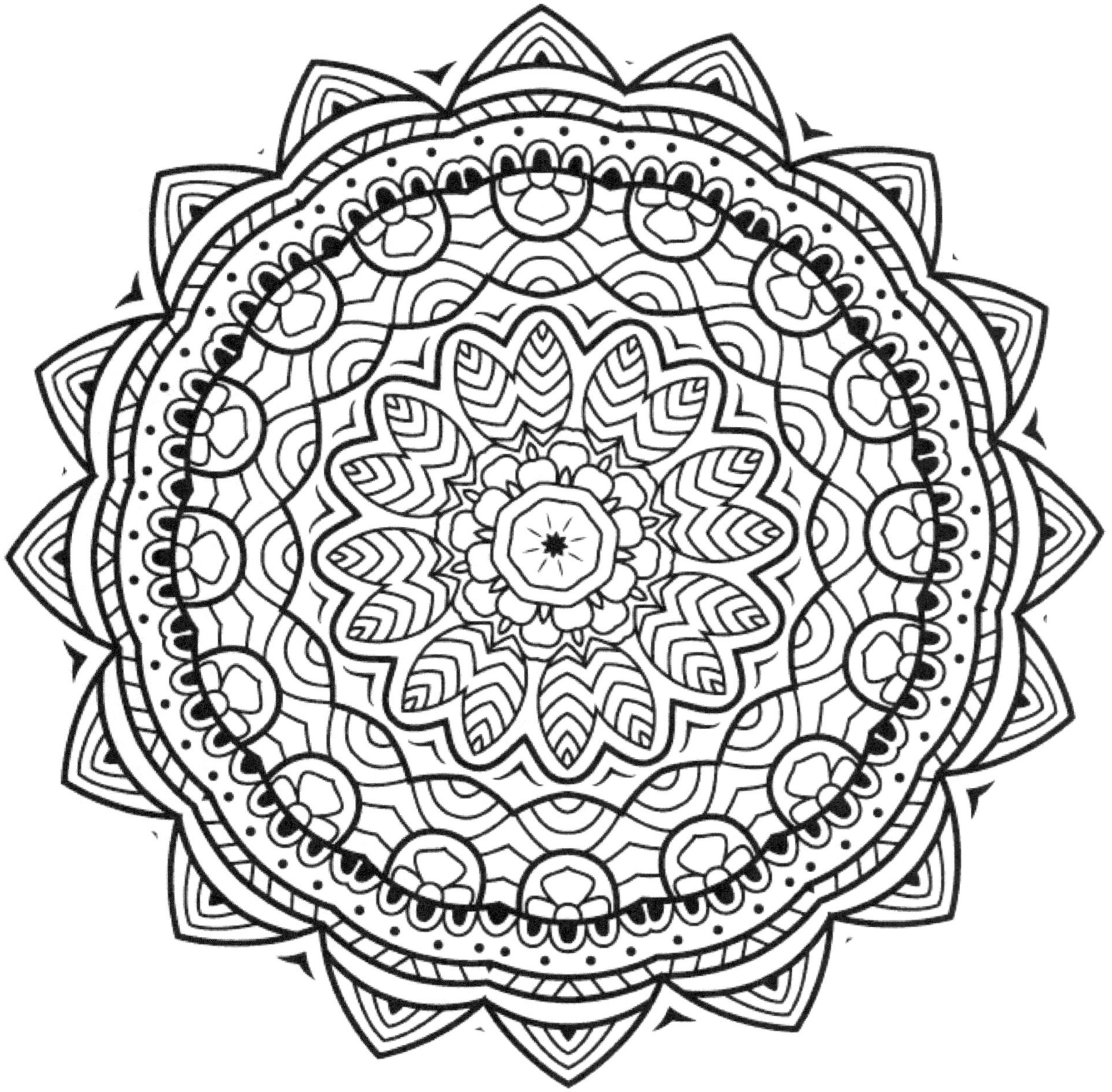

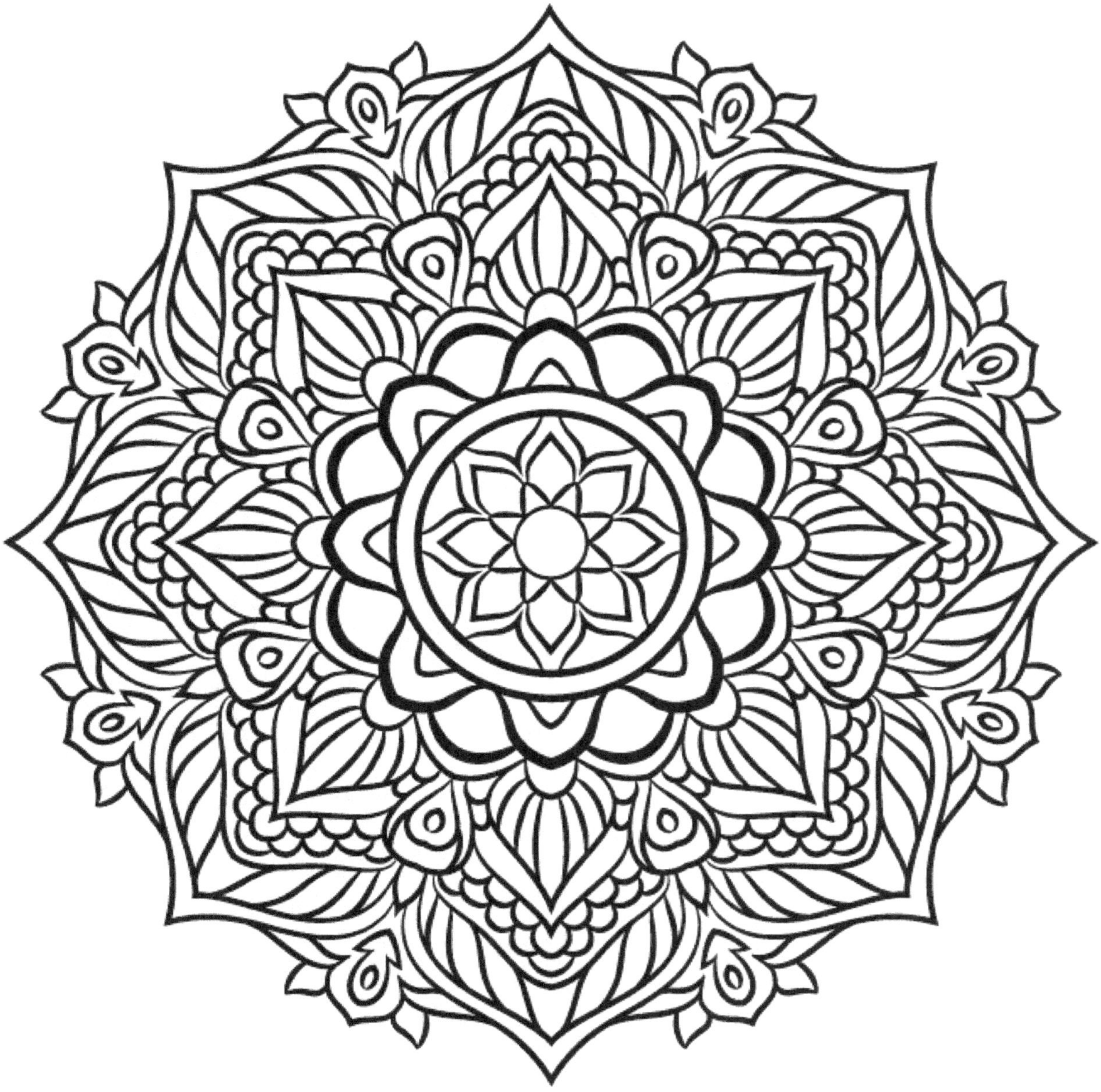

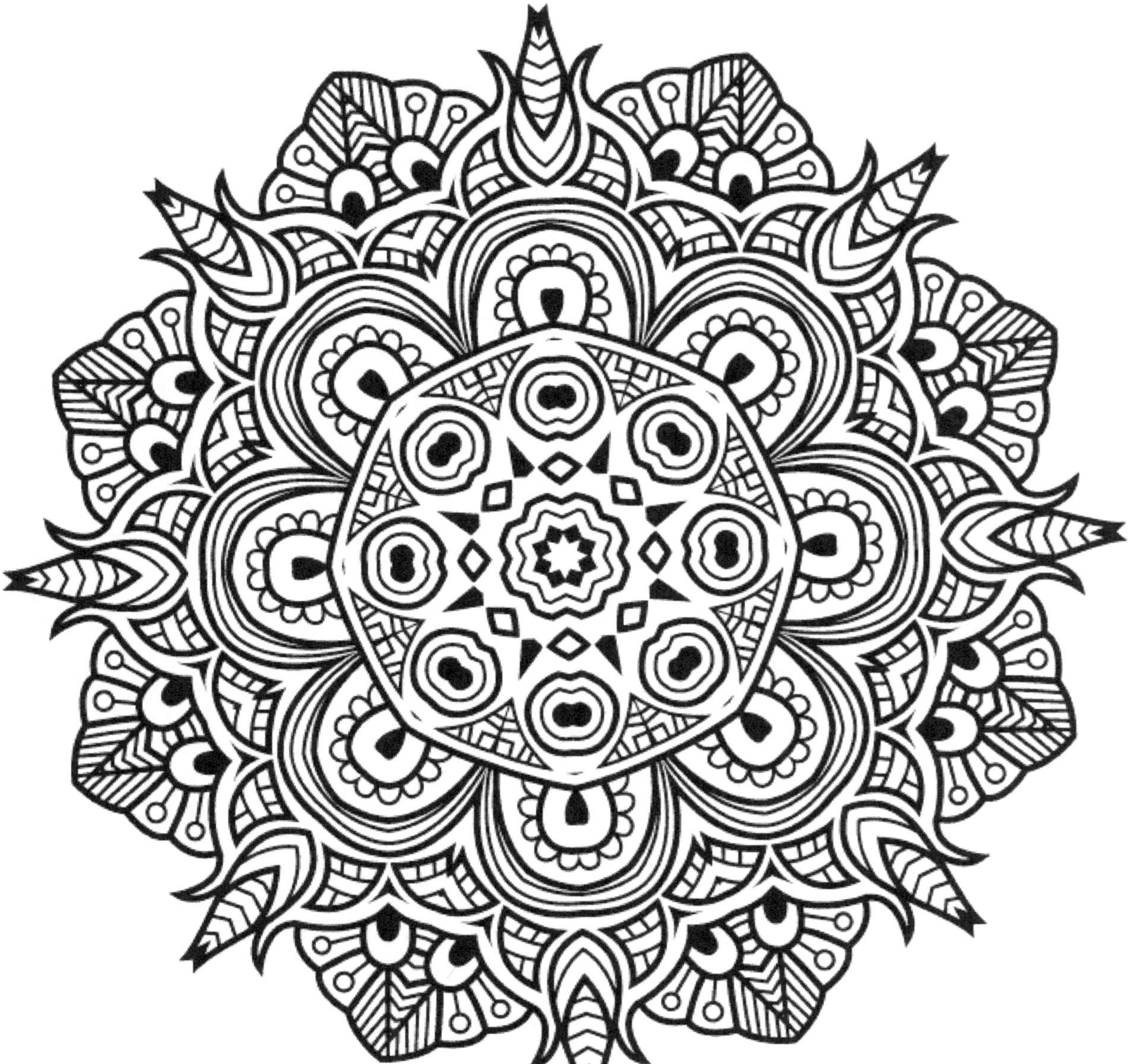

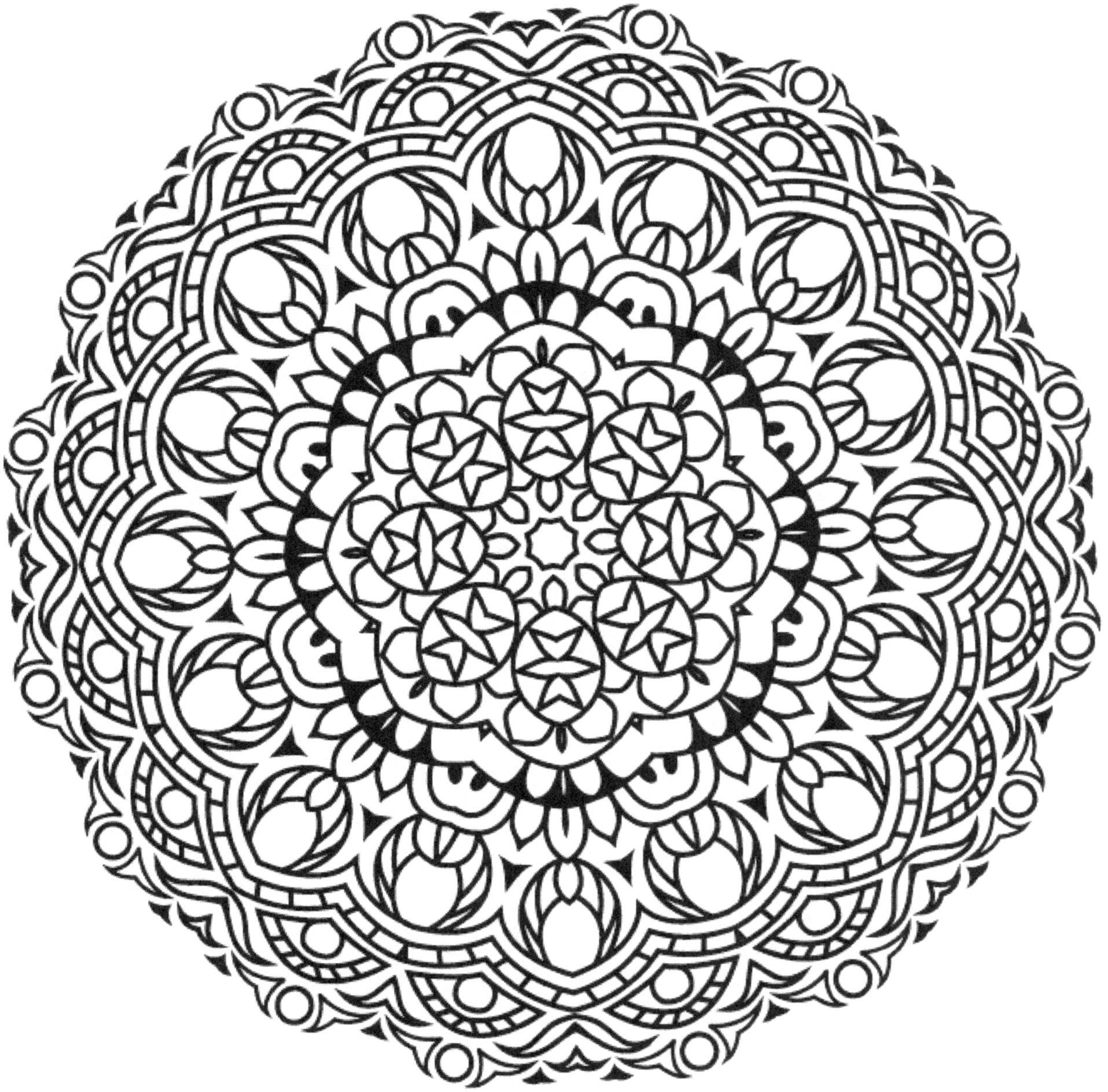

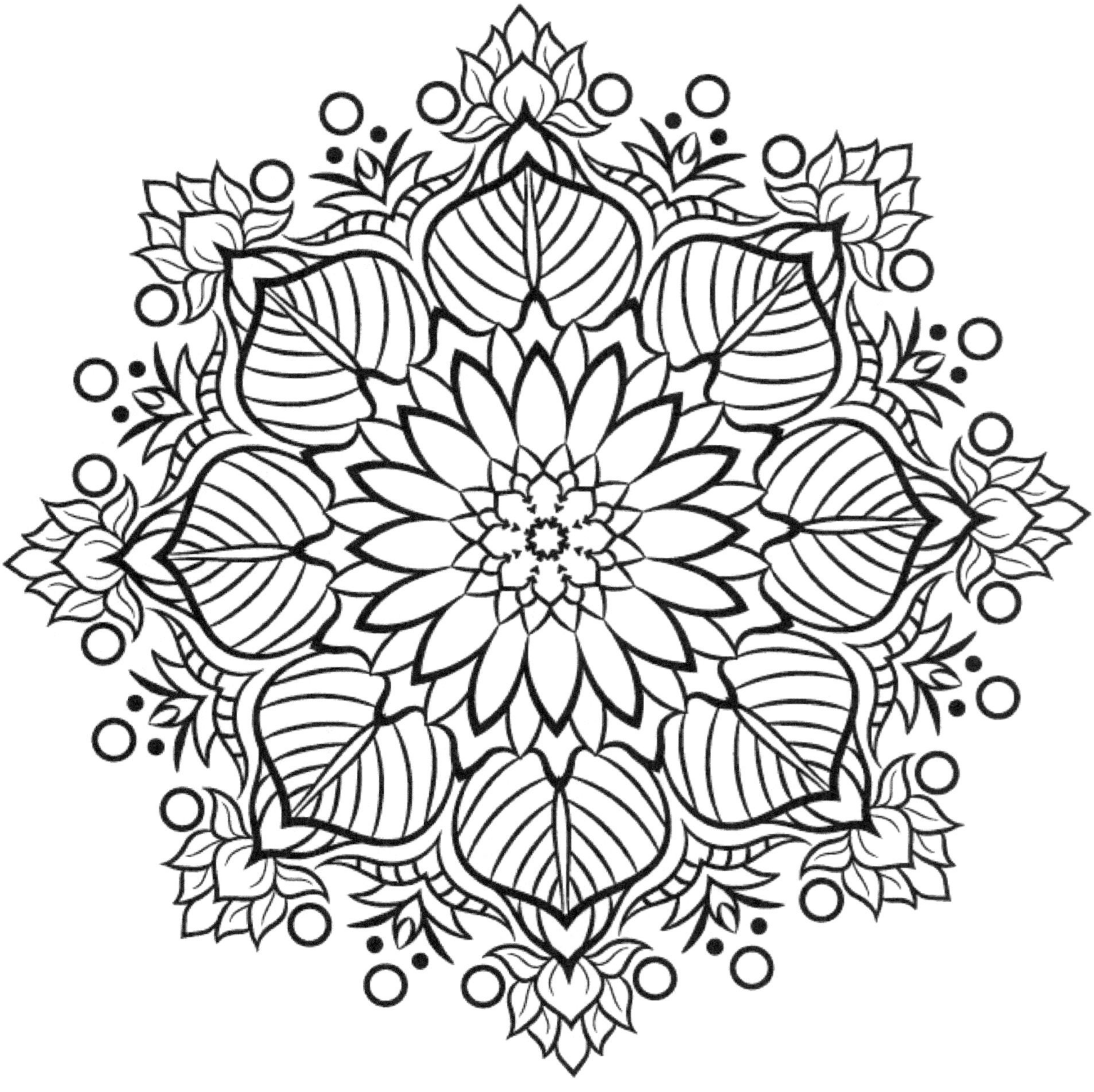

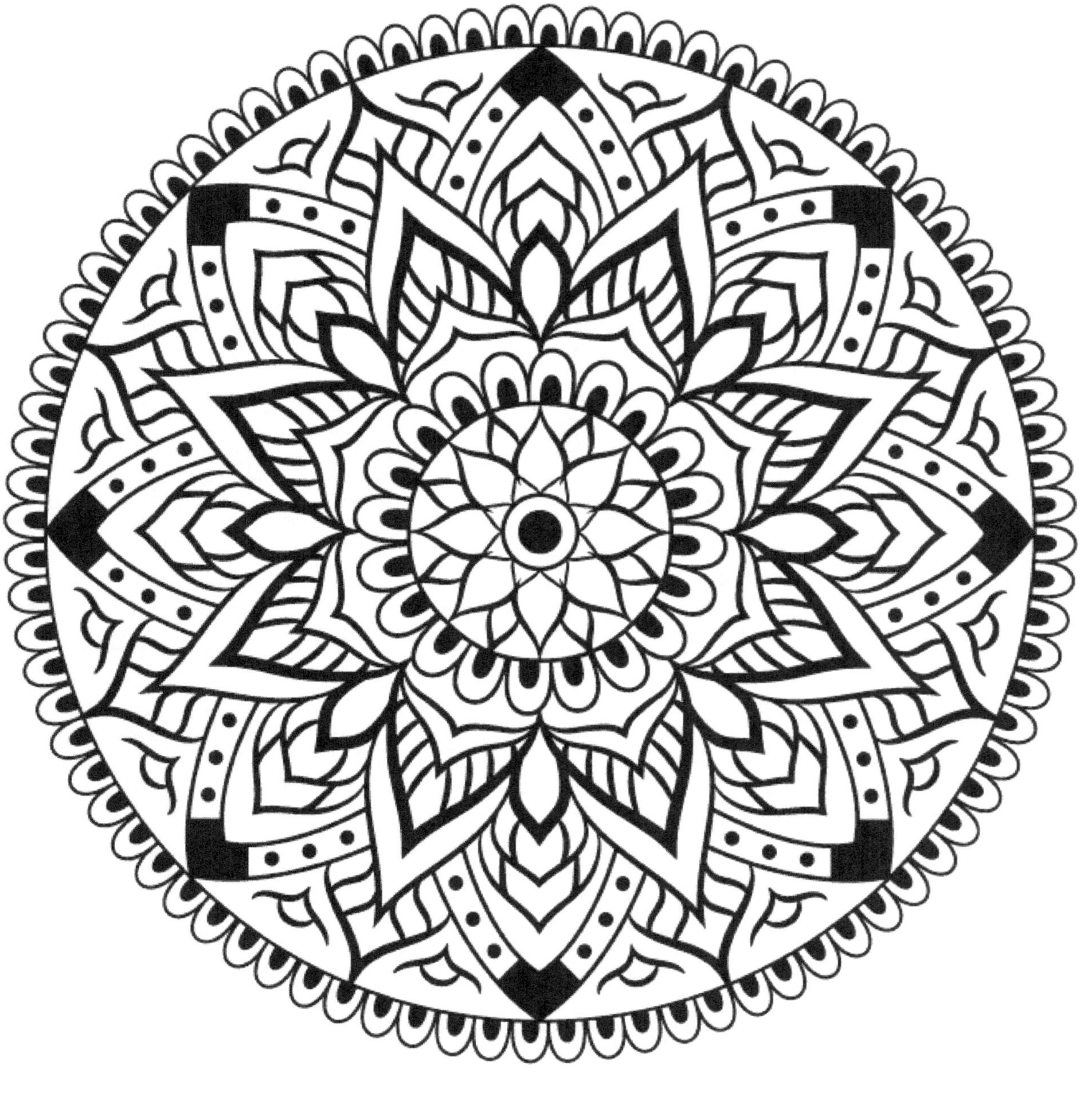

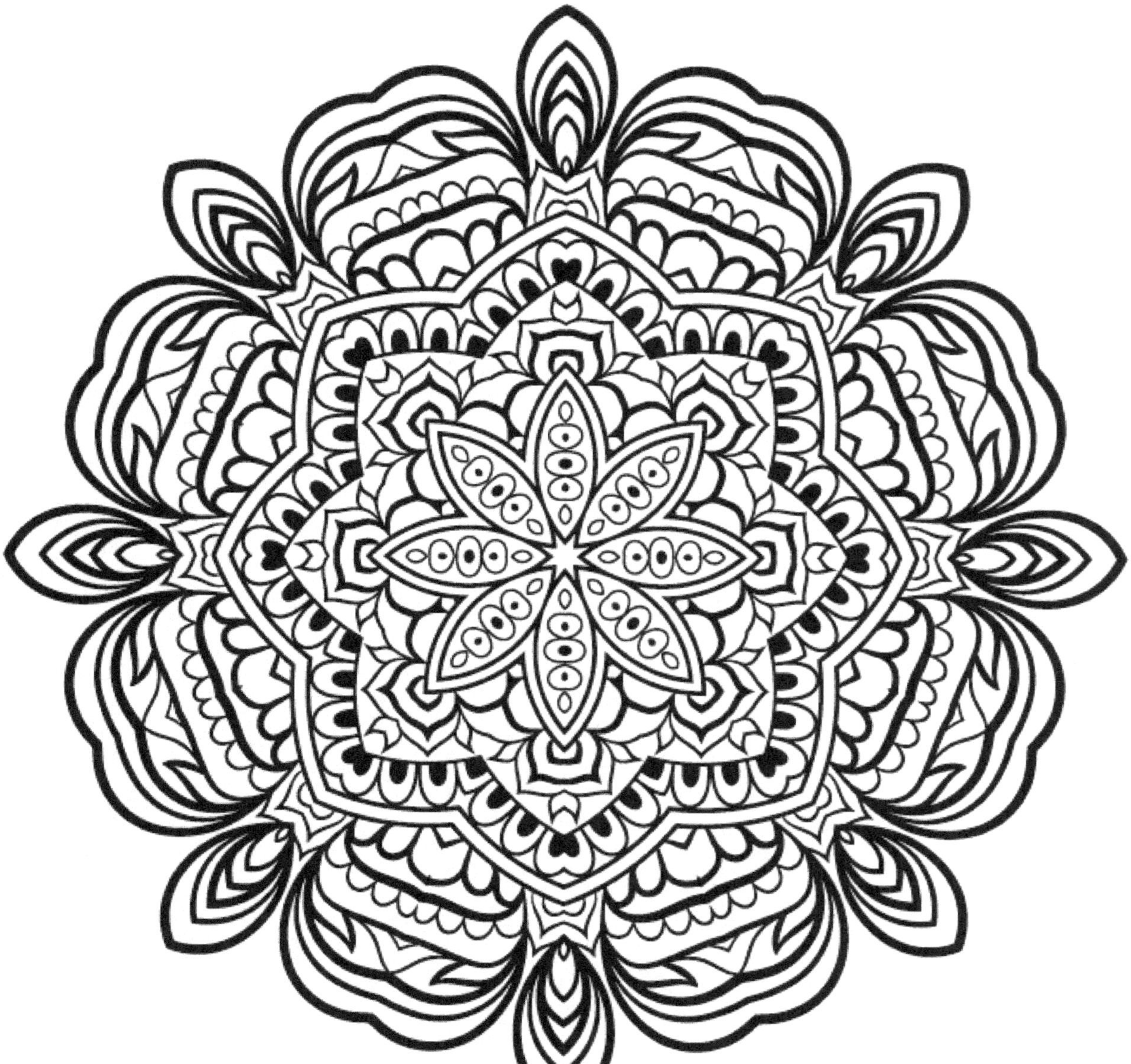

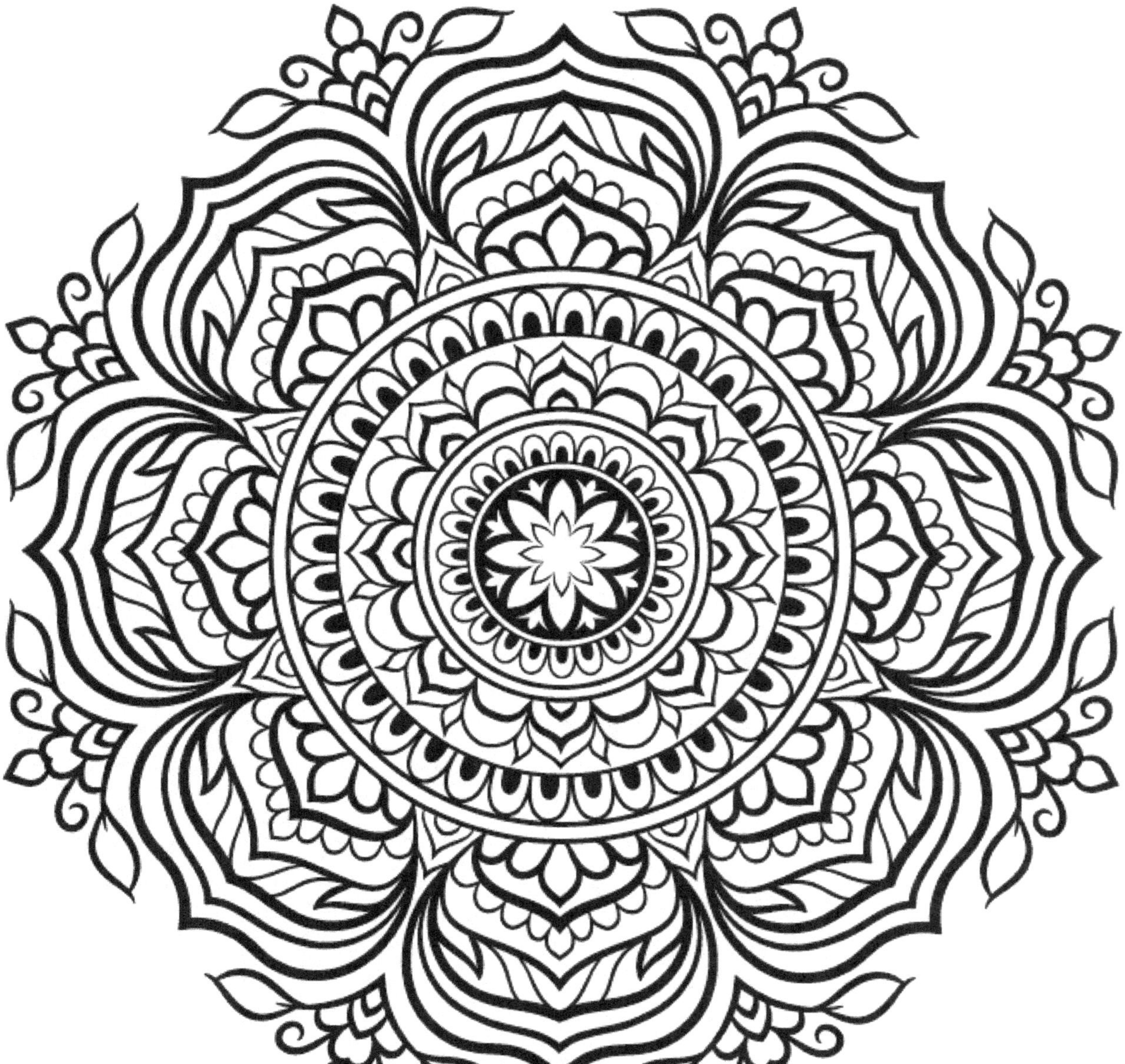

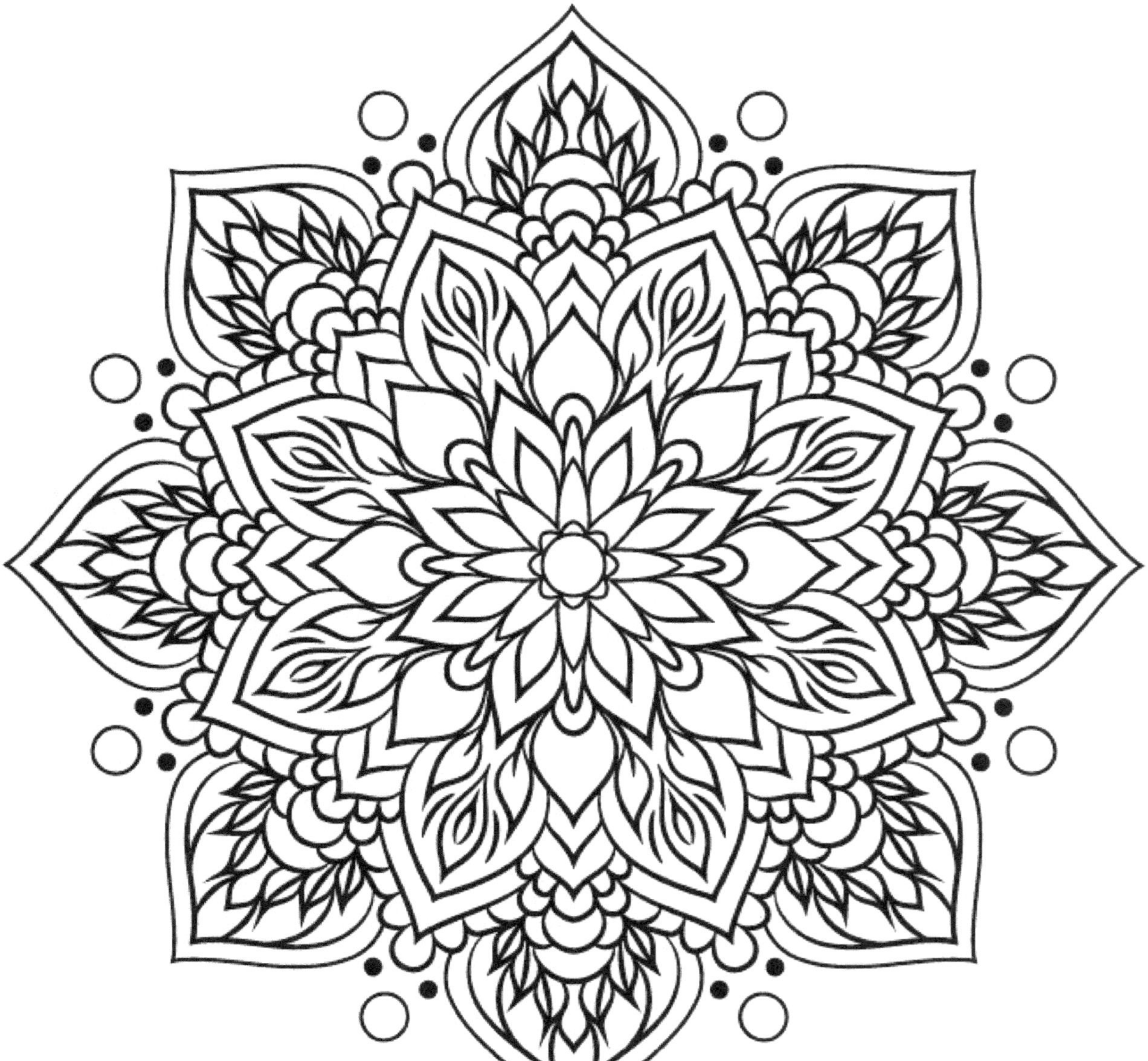

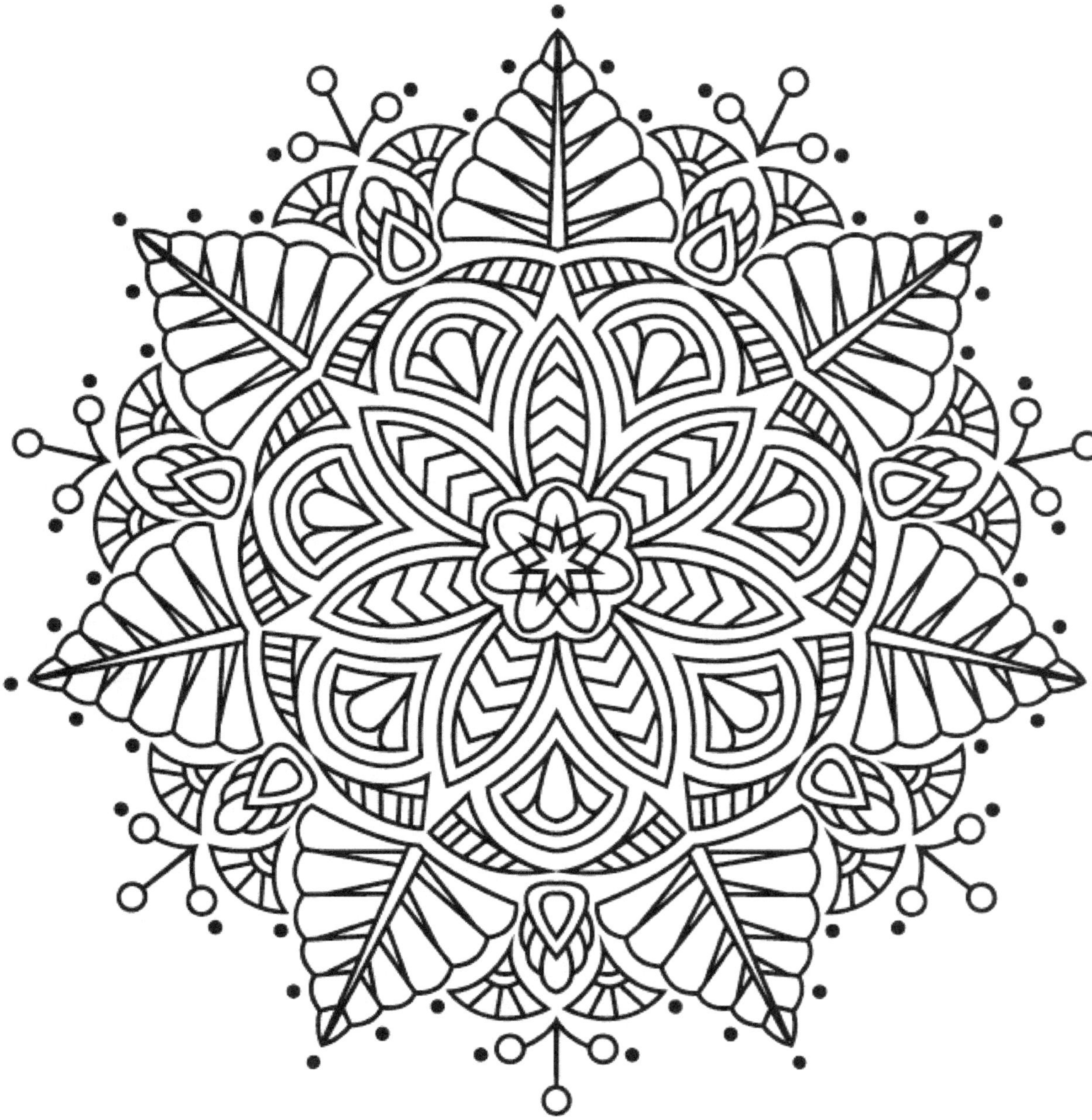

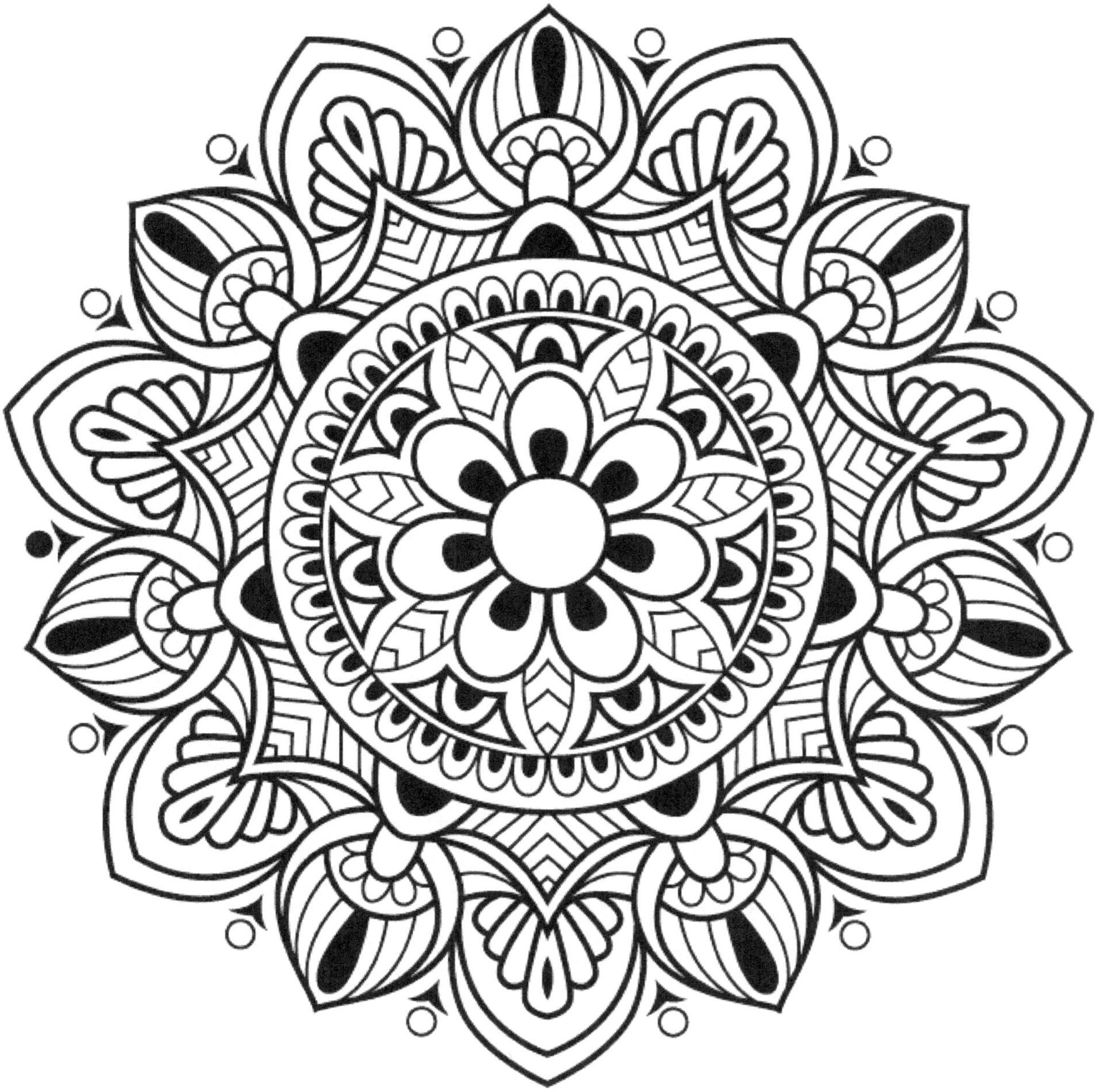

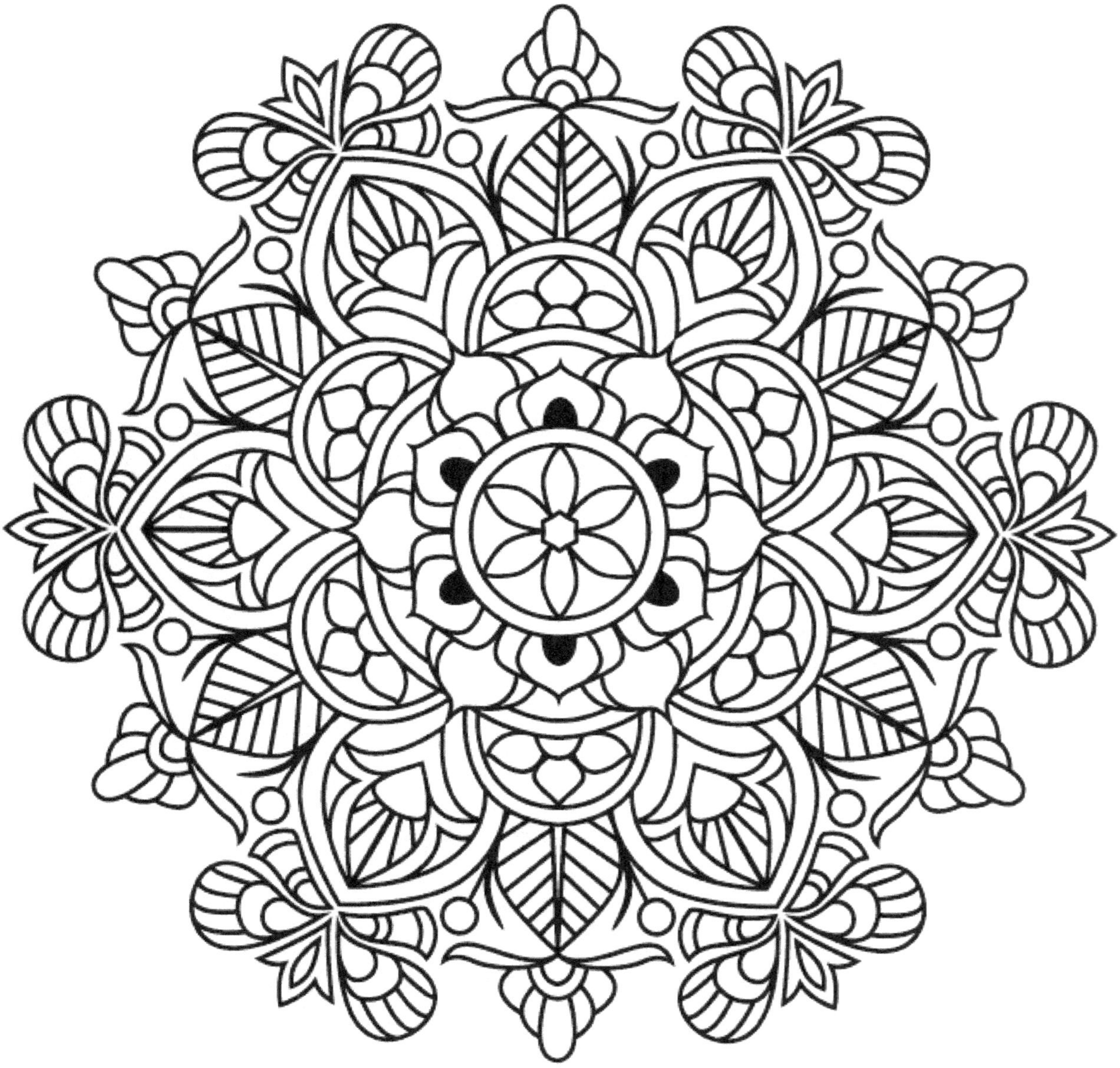

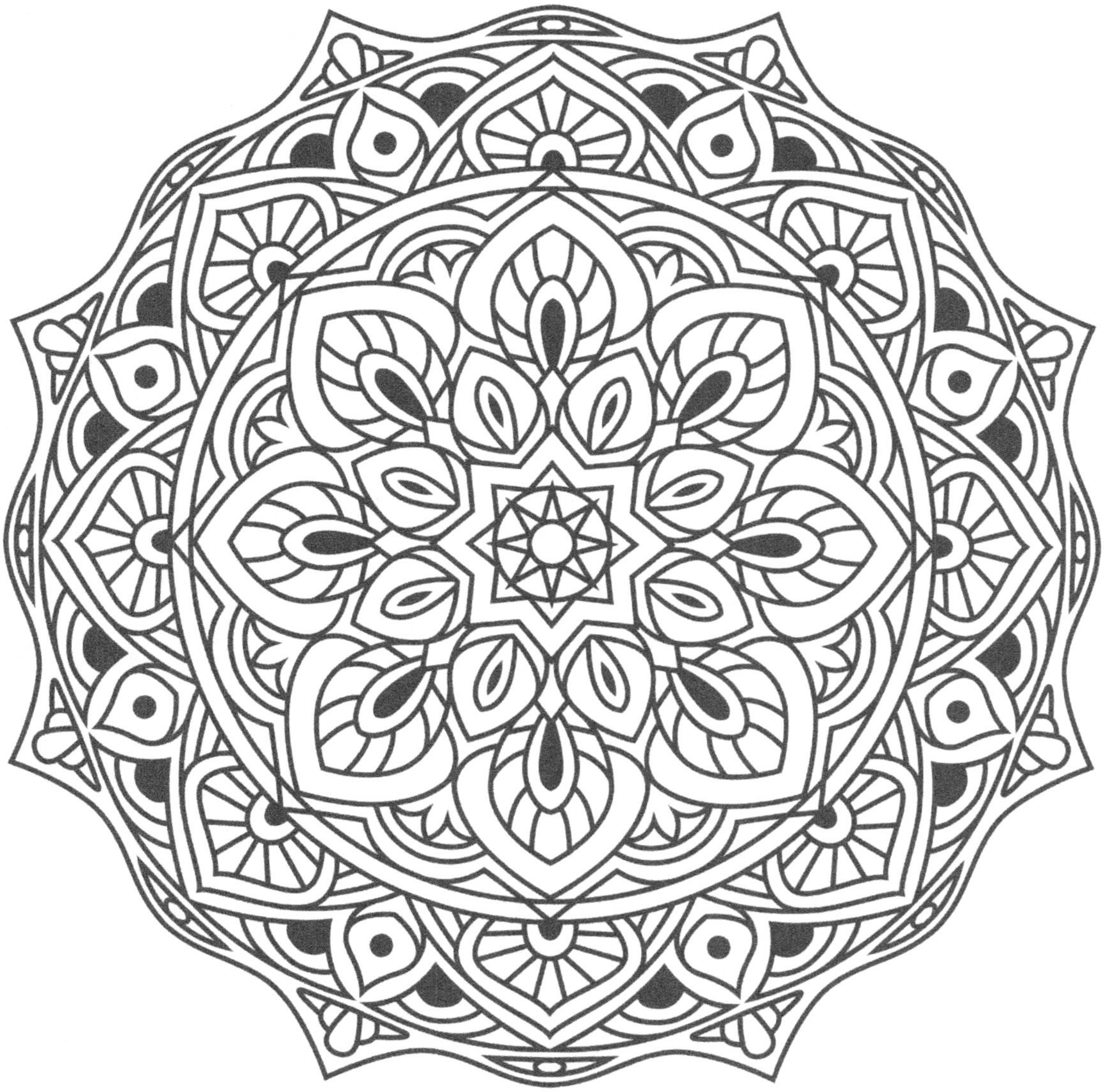

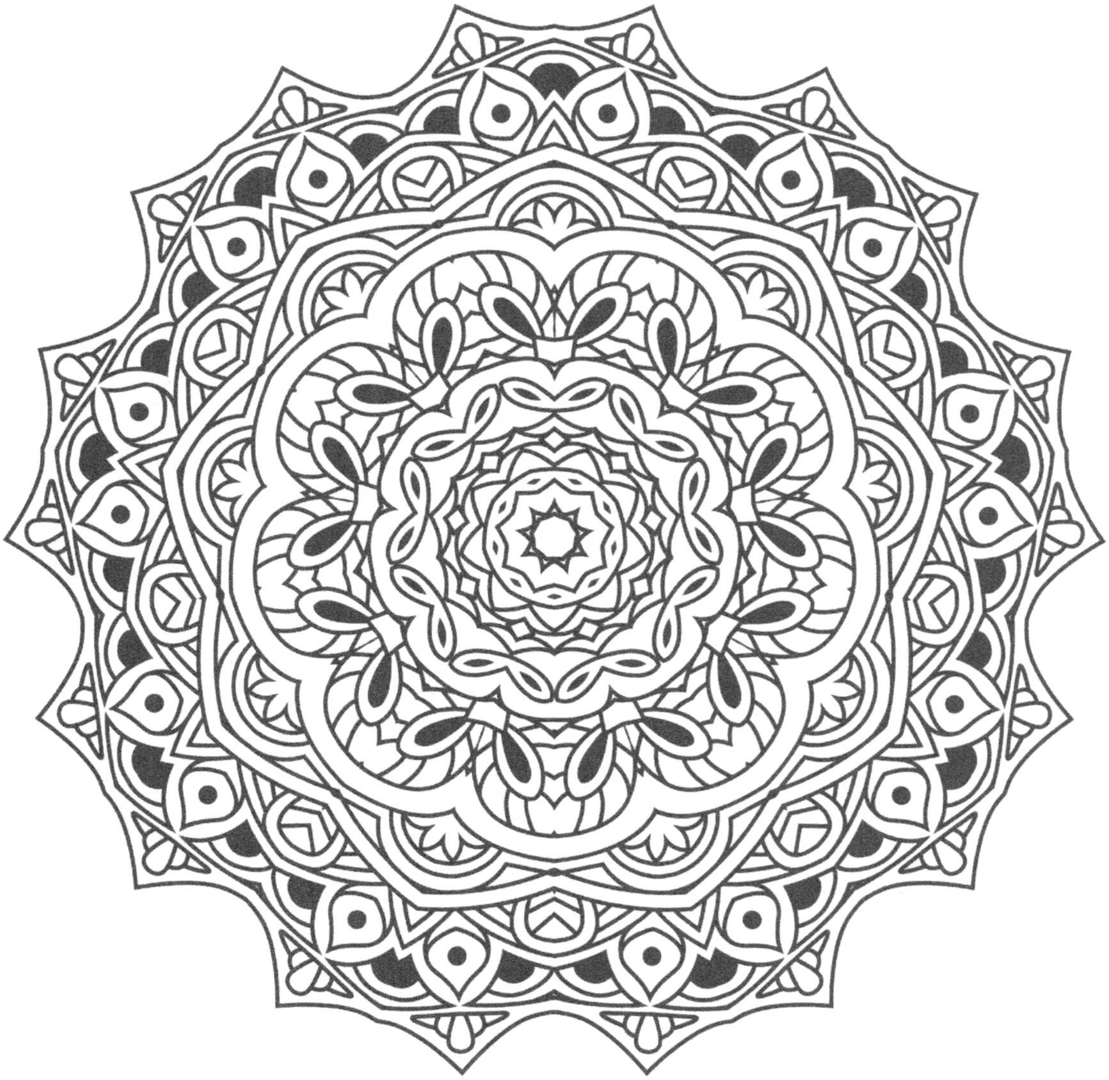

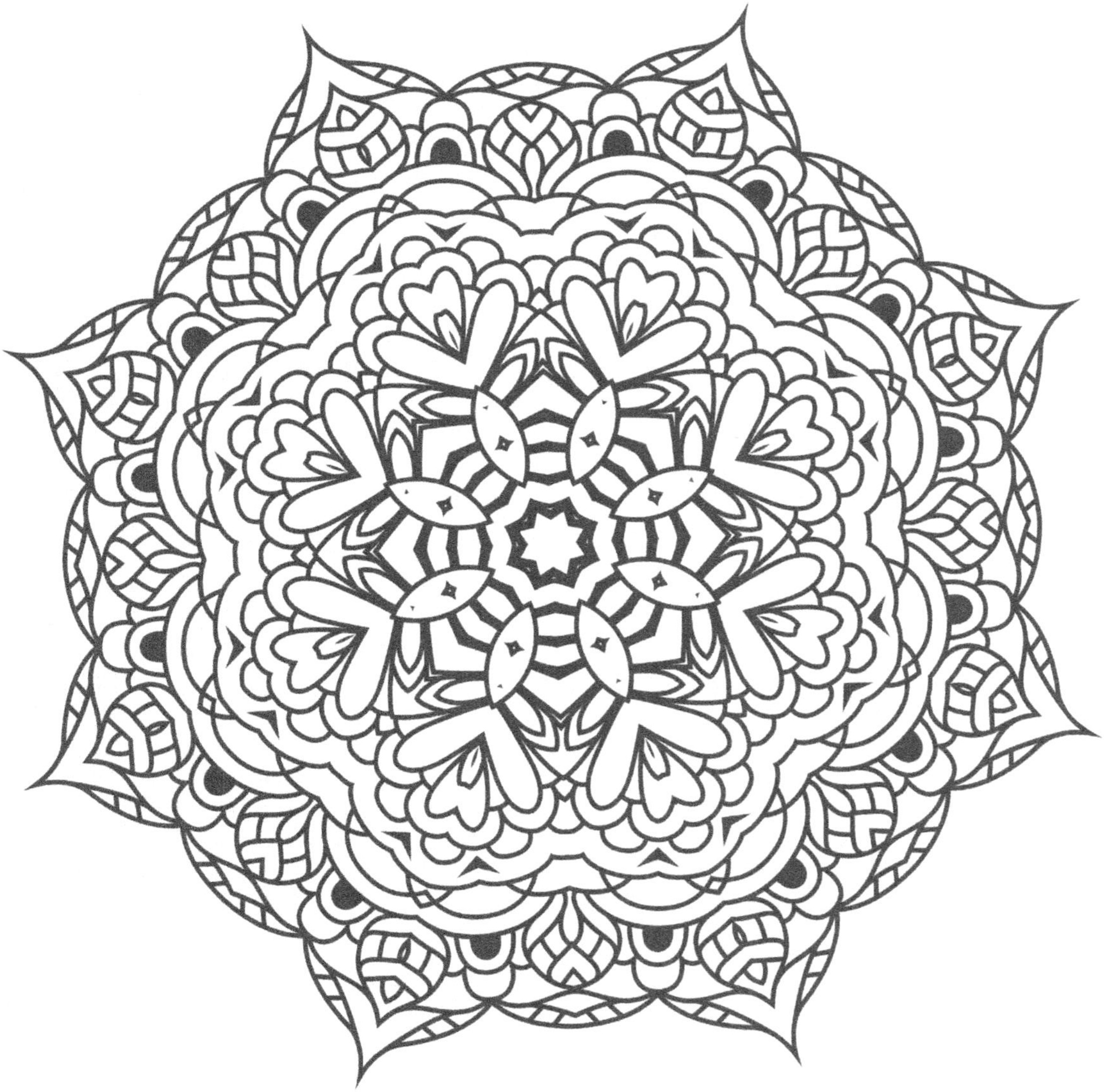

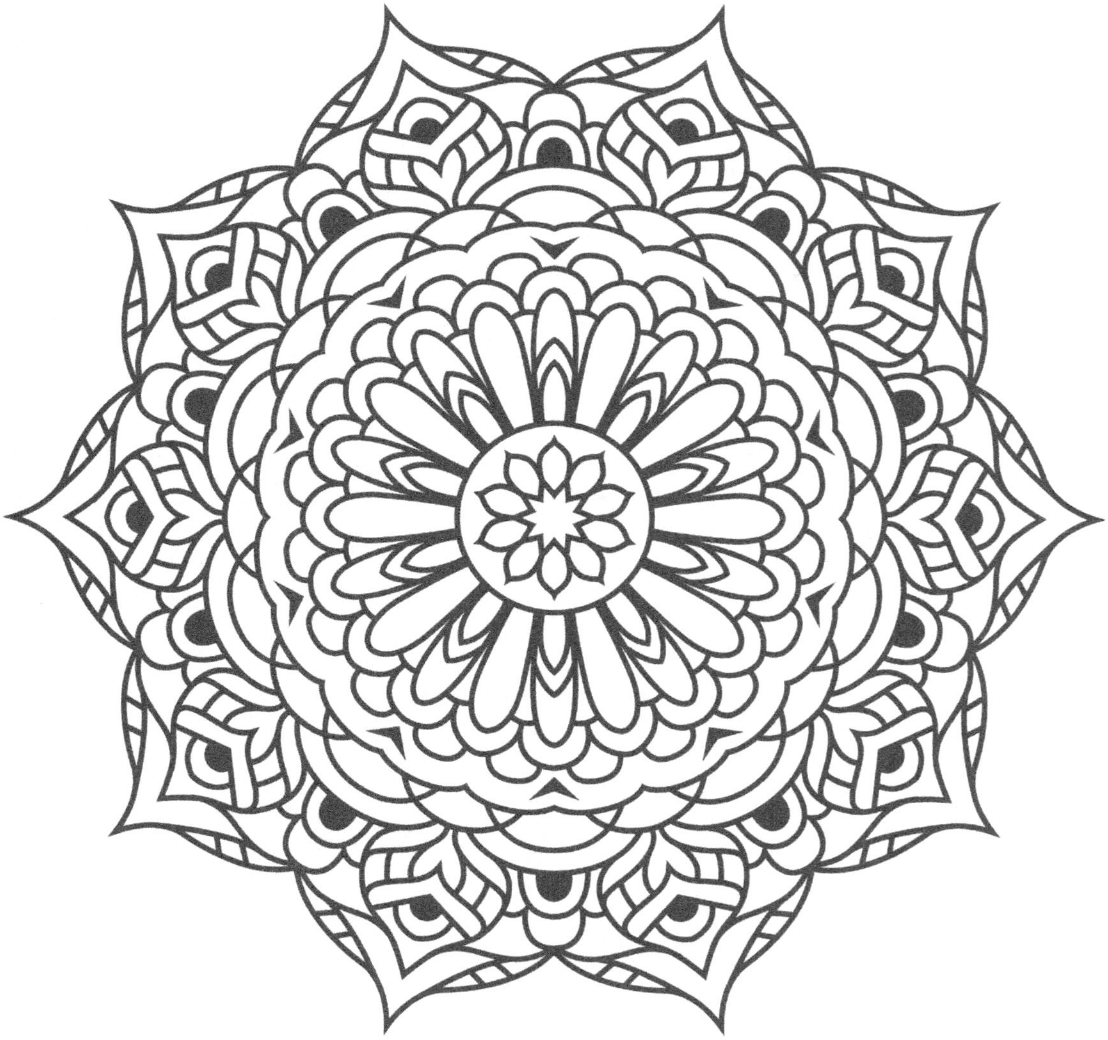

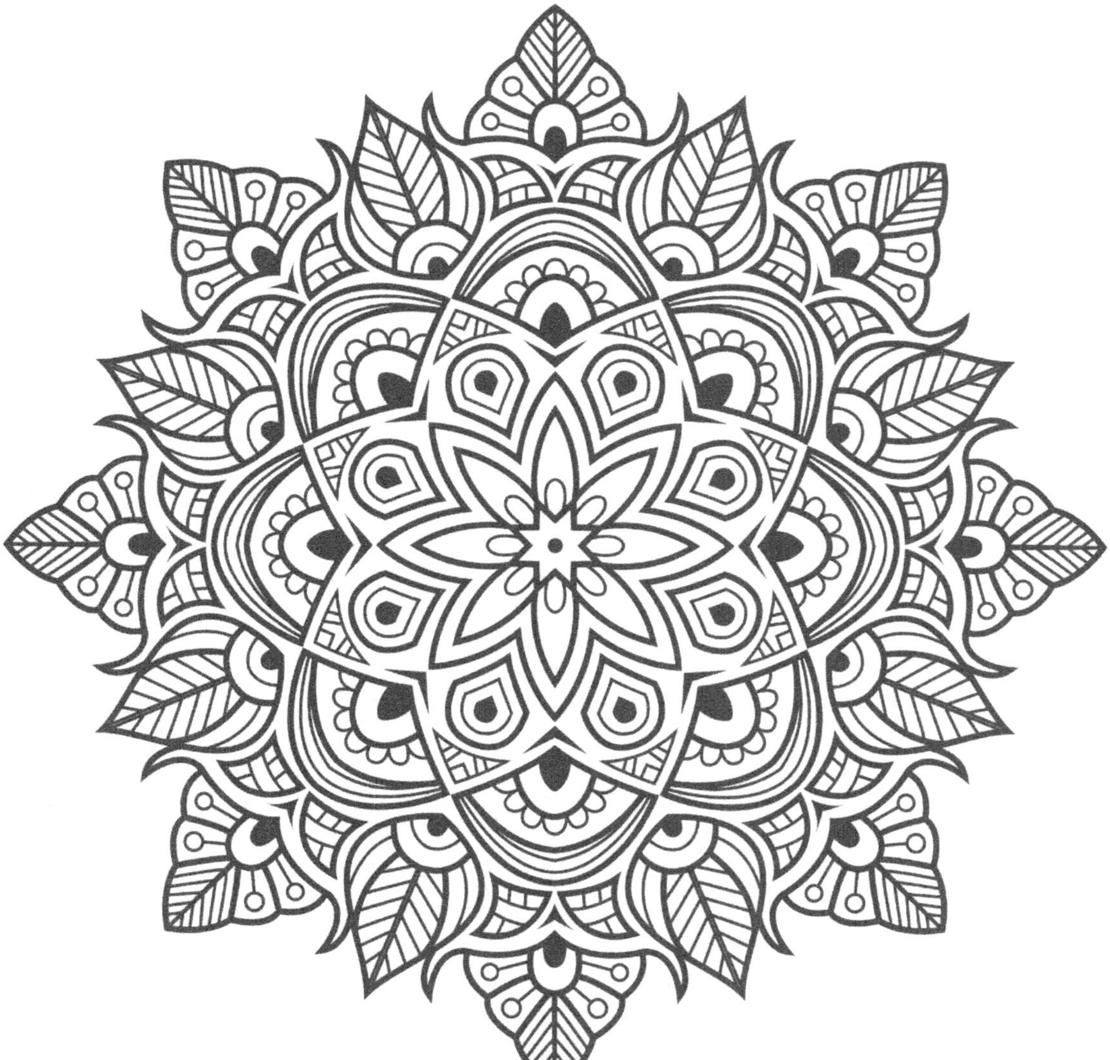

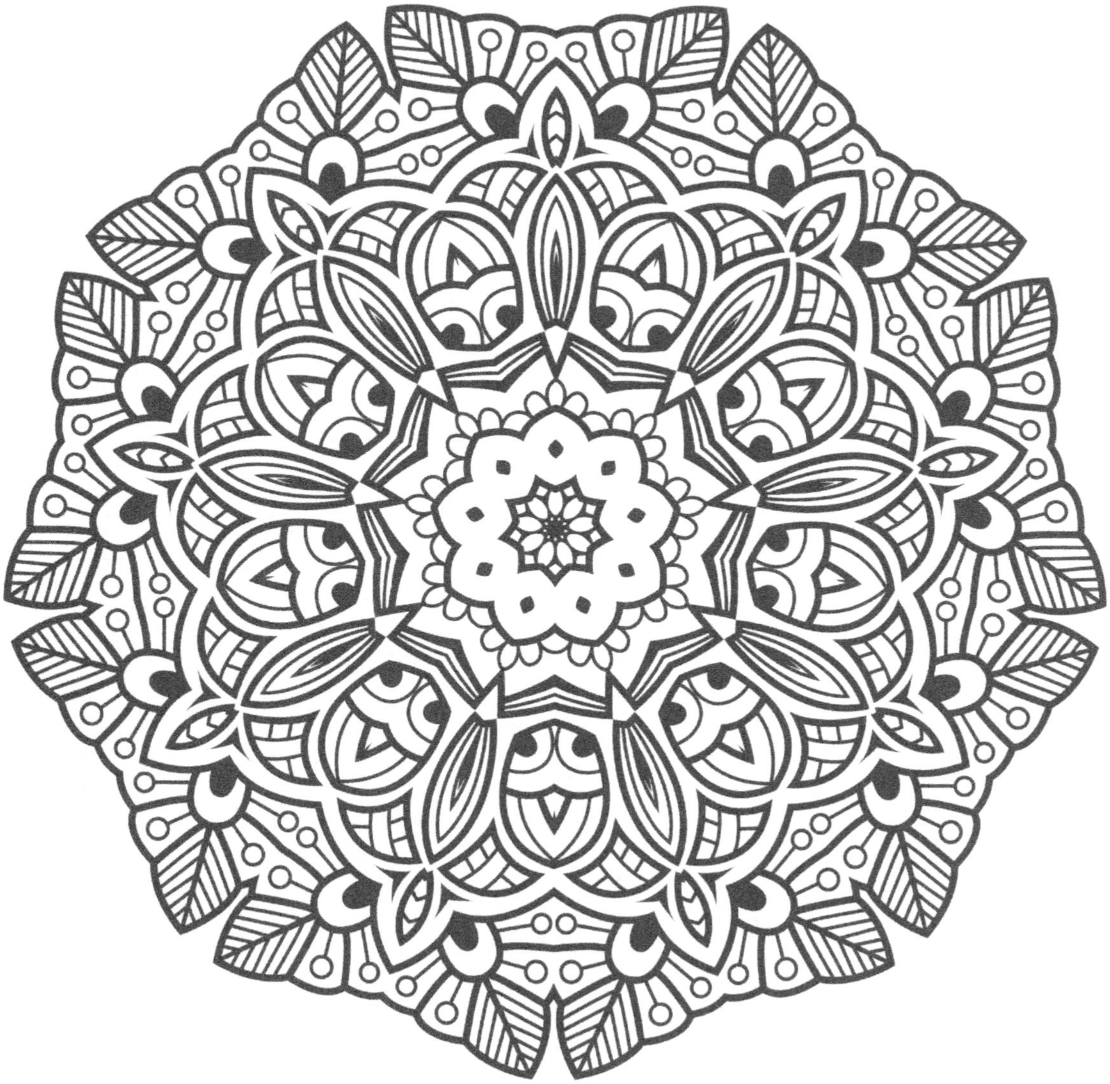

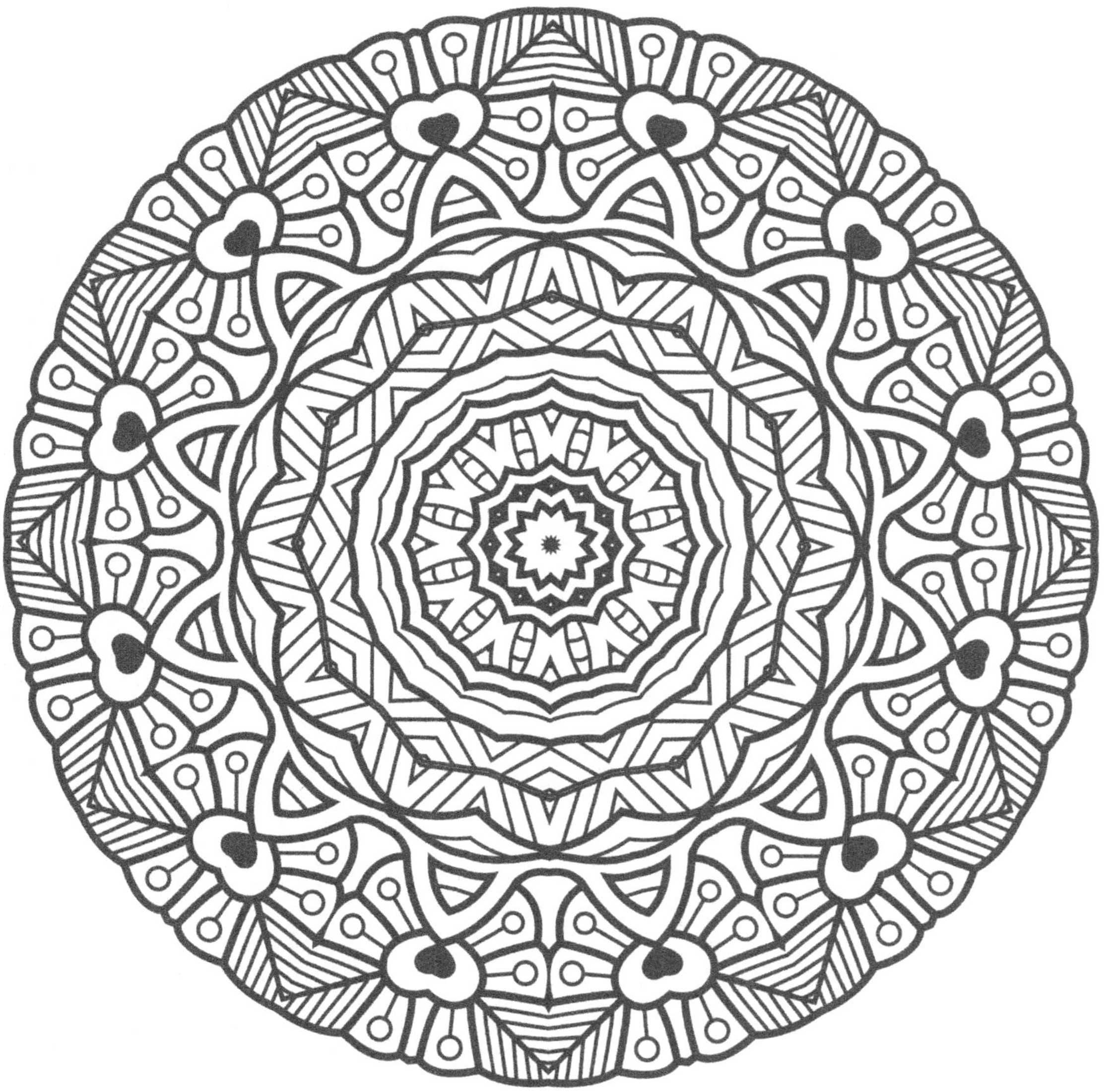

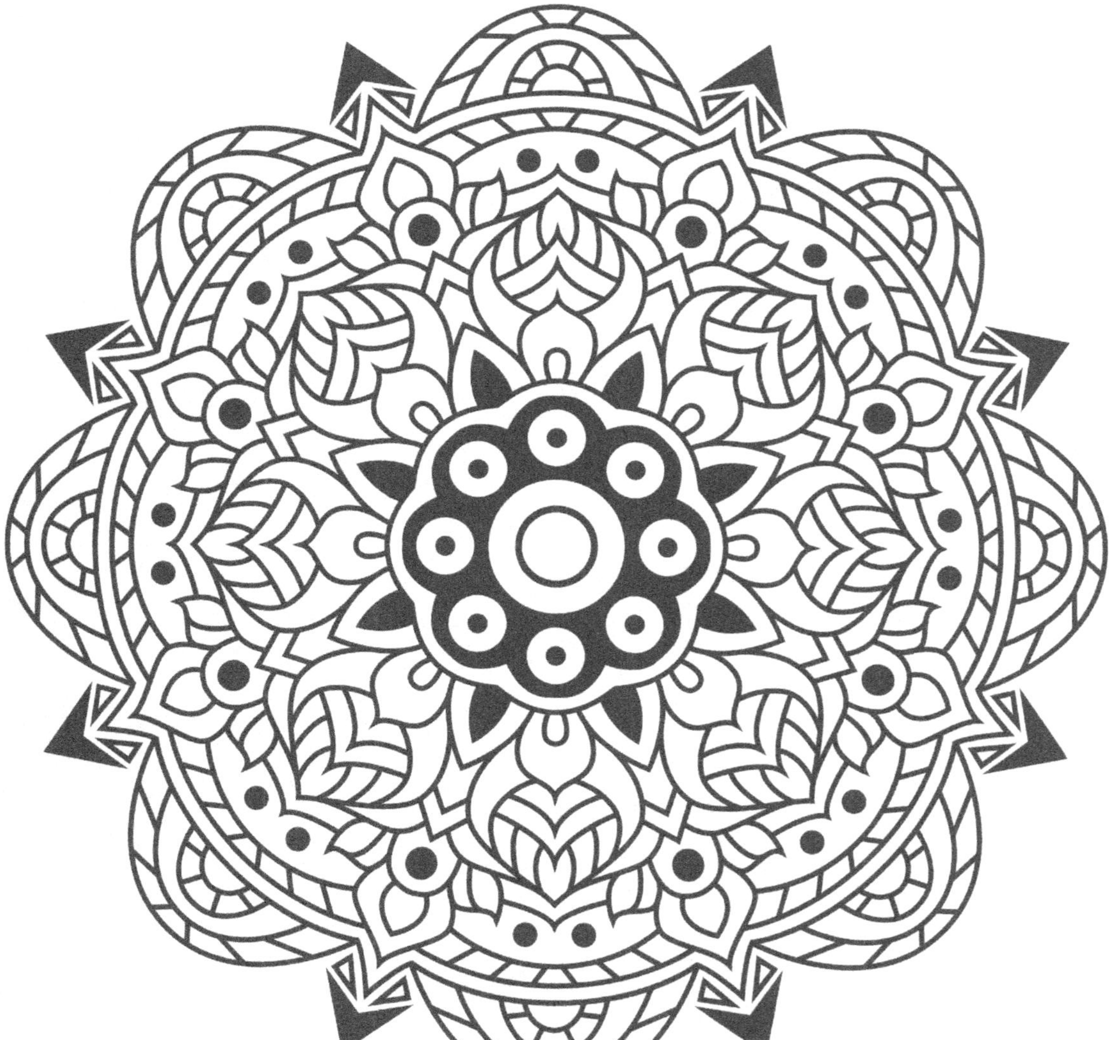

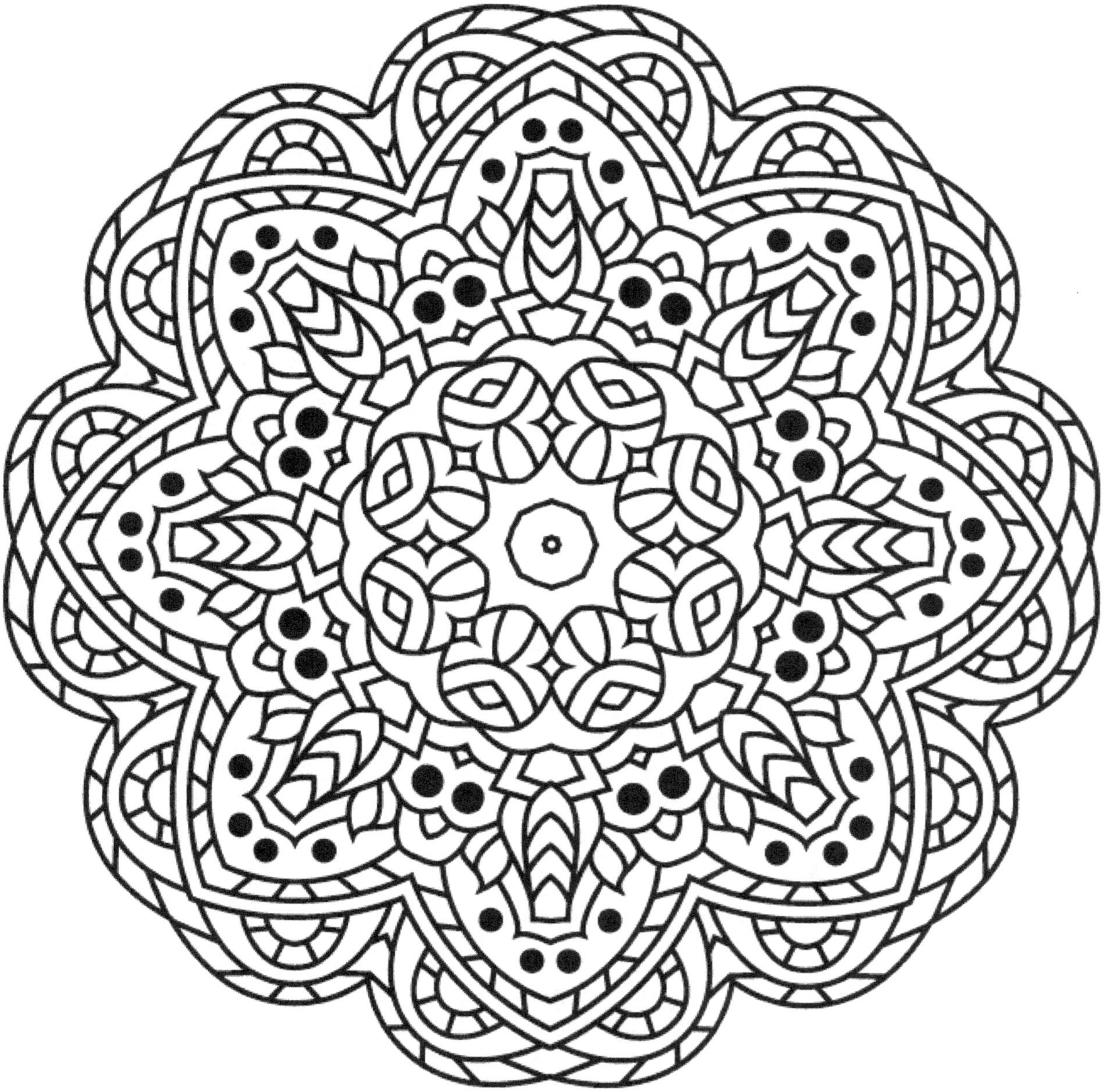

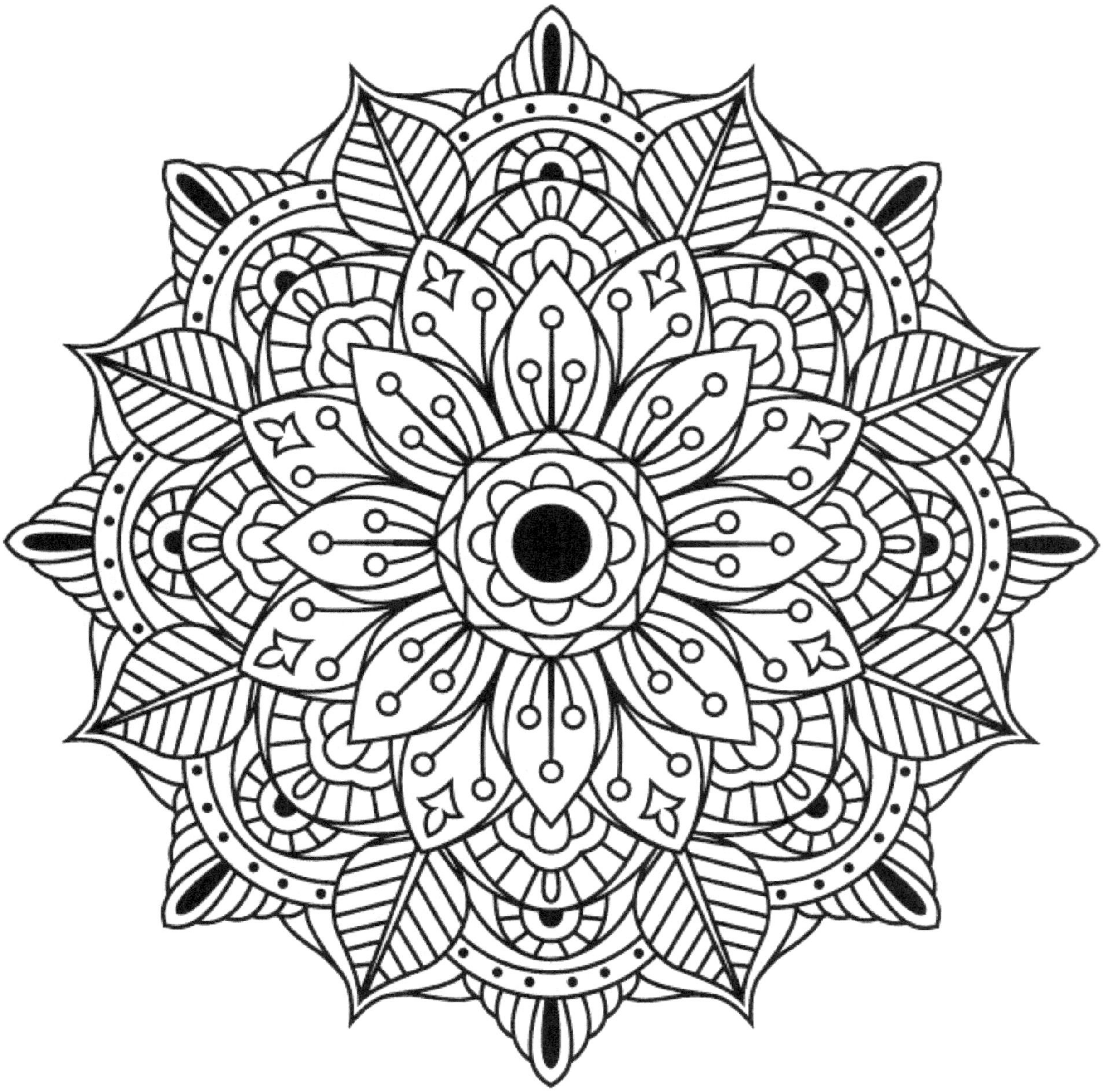

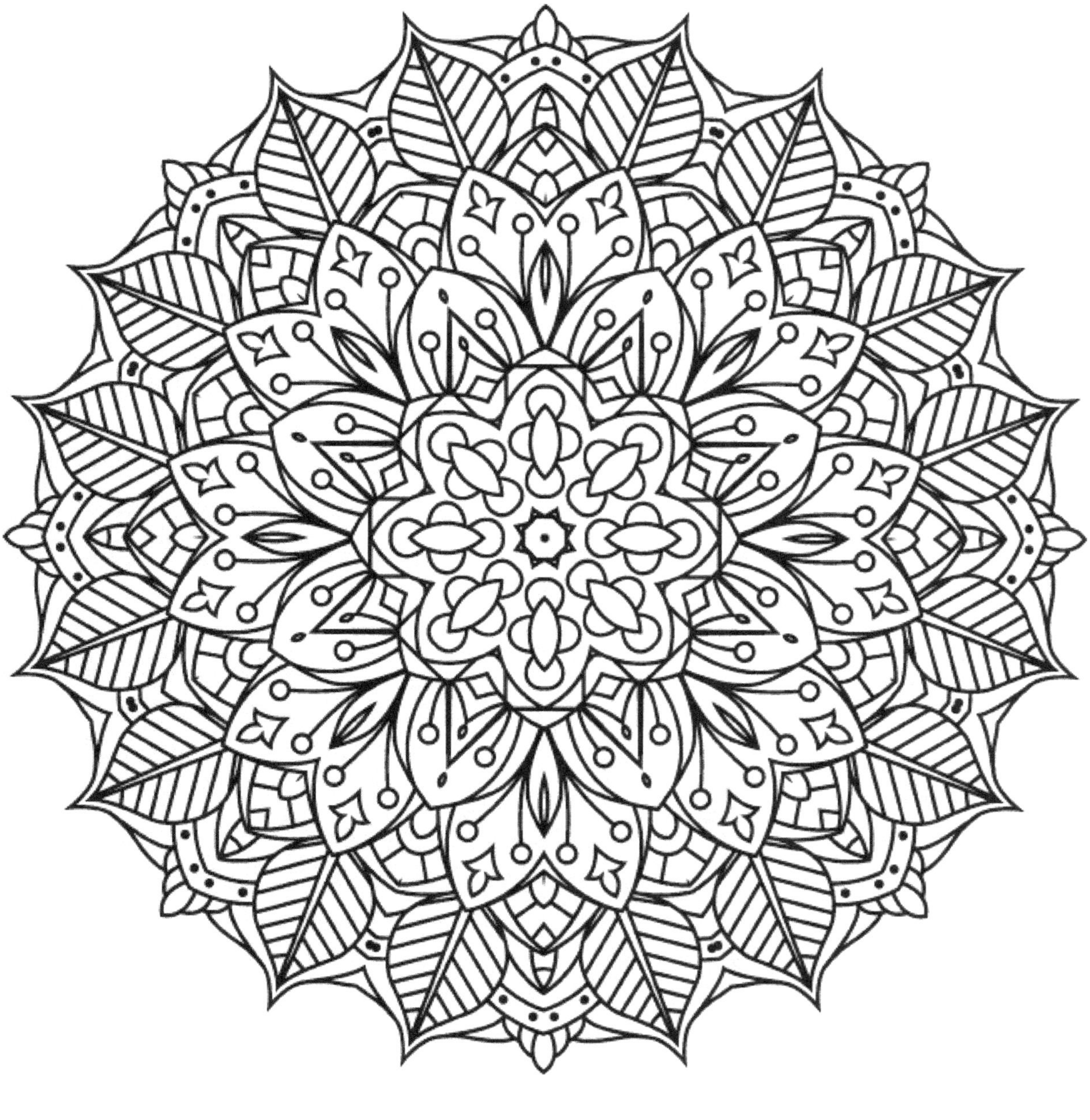

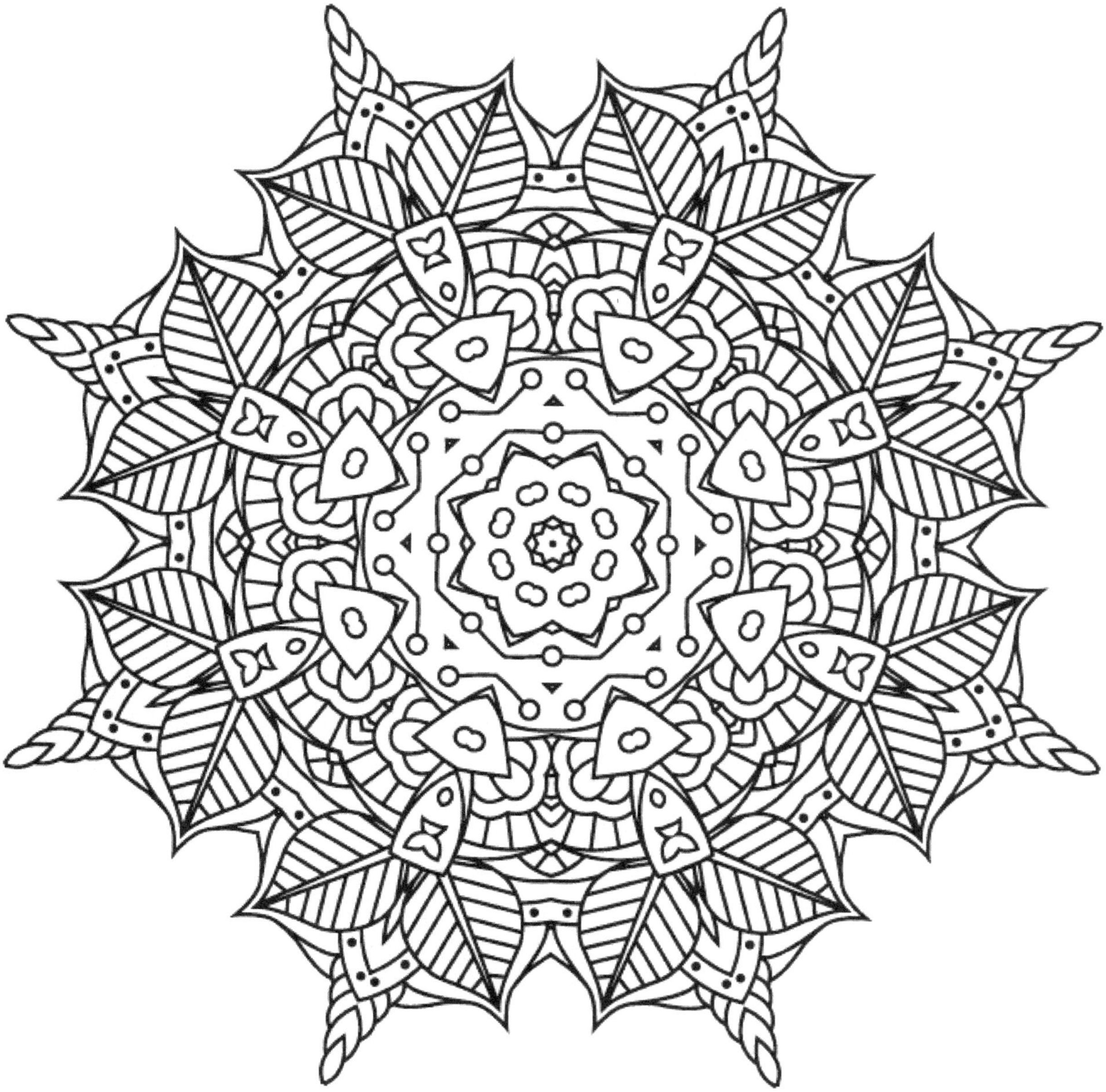

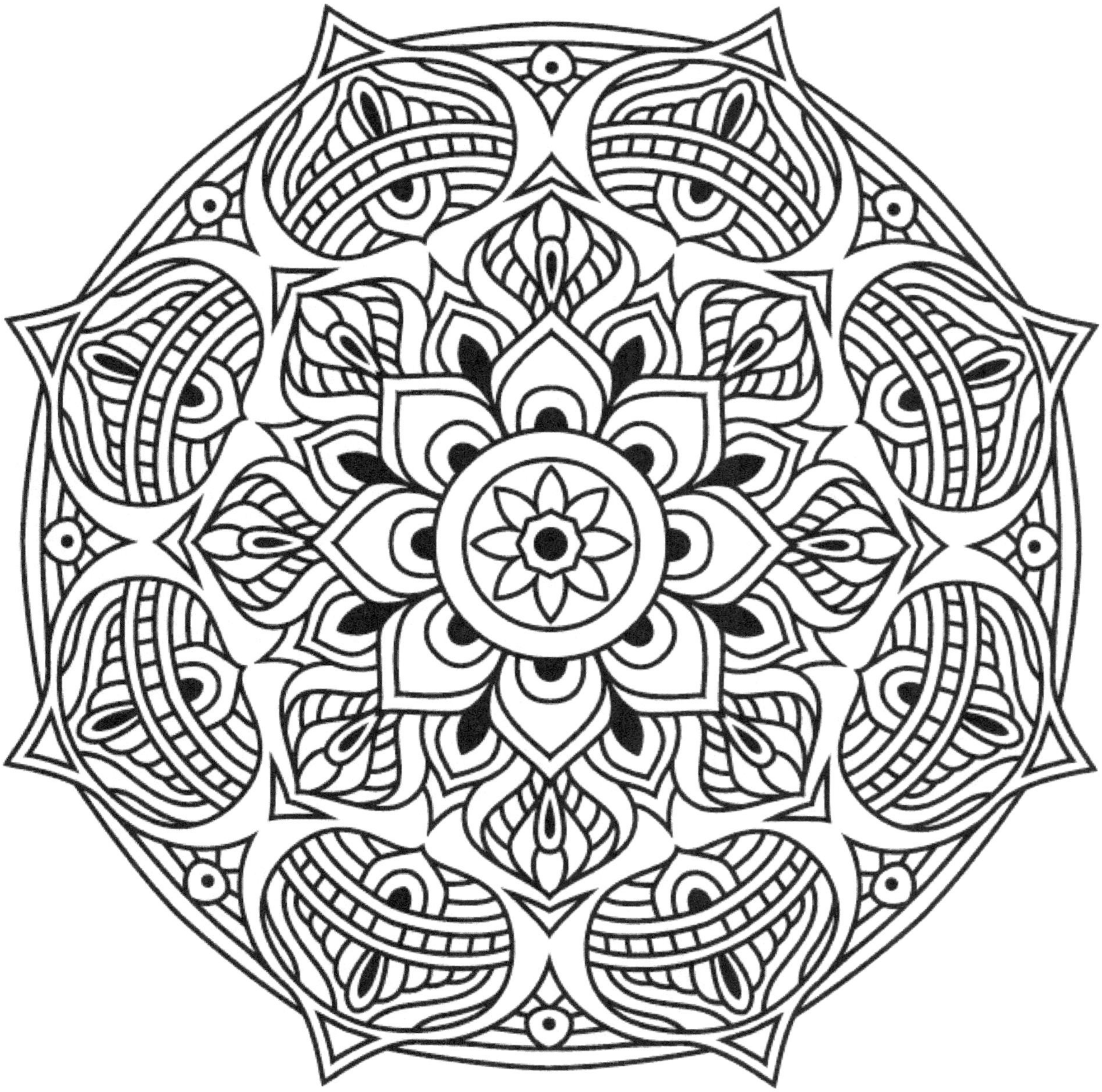

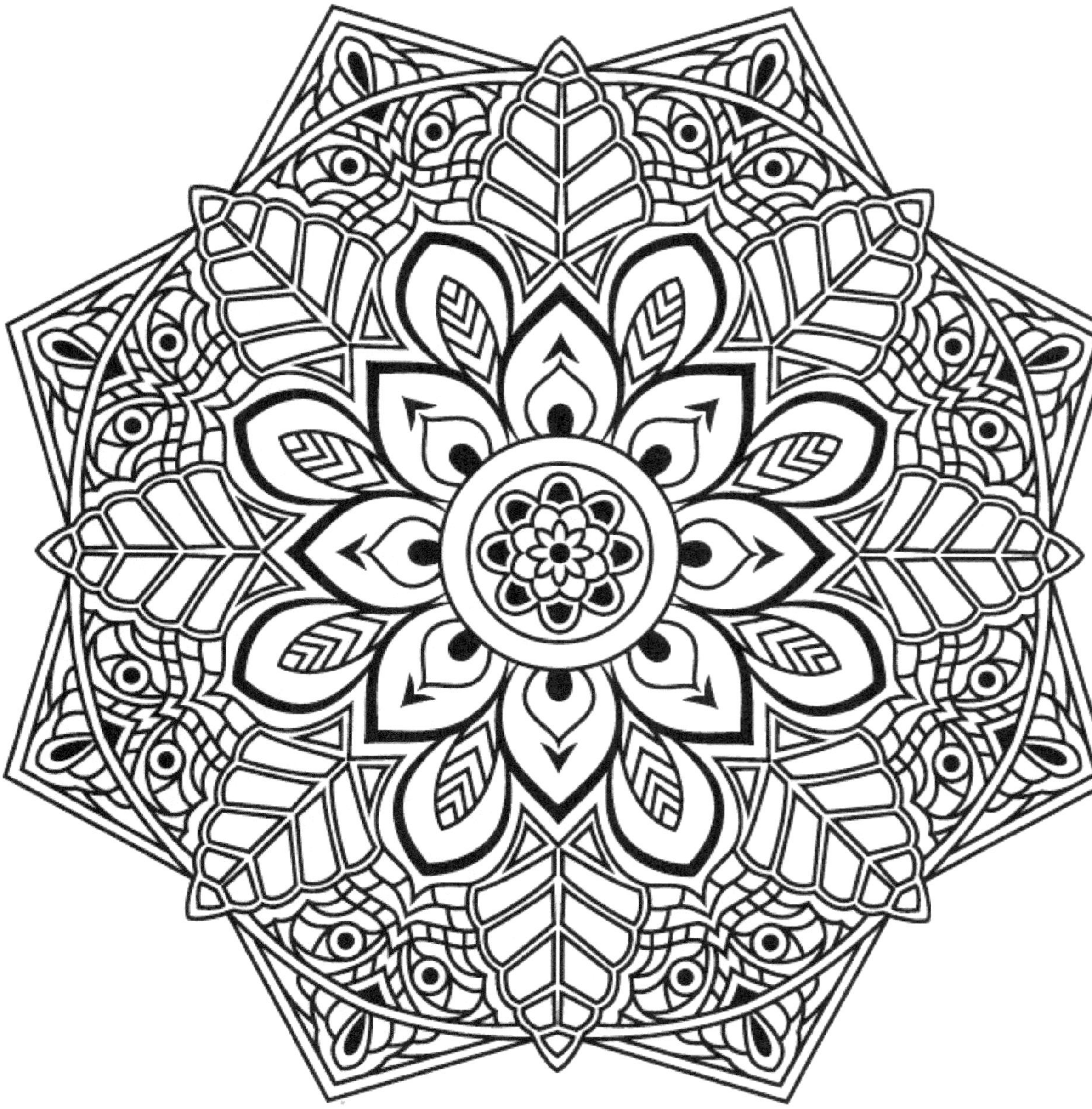

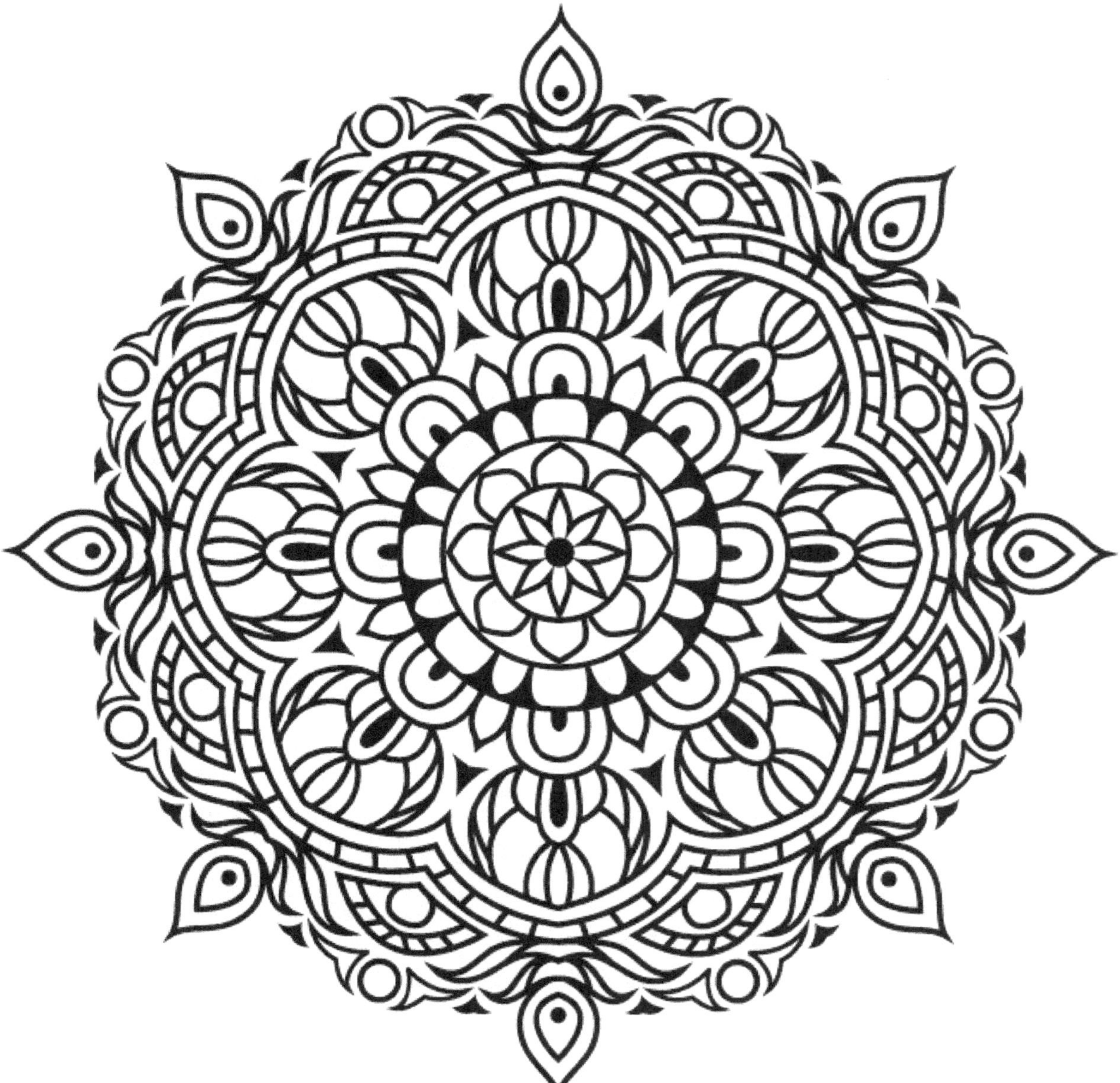

www.ingramcontent.com/pod-product-compliance
Lightning Source LLC
Chambersburg PA
CBHW081630220526
45468CB00009B/2380
9781724401557